Friends

Making Them & Keeping Them

by Patti Kelley Criswell

illustrated by Stacy Peterson

★ American Girl®

Questions or comments? Call 1-800-845-0005,
visit our Web site at **americangirl.com,**
or write to Customer Service, American Girl, 8400 Fairway Place, Middleton, WI 53562-0497.

Printed in China
08 09 10 11 12 LEO 15 14 13 12 11

All American Girl marks are trademarks of American Girl, LLC.

Editorial Development: Michelle Watkins, Erin Falligant

Art Direction & Design: Chris Lorette David

Styling: Camela Decaire

Production: Mindy Rappe, Kendra Schluter, Jeannette Bailey, Judith Lary

Illustrations: Stacy Peterson

Dear Reader,

At American Girl, we understand how important it is to have friends you can count on.

Inside, we've given you everything you need to know about **making new friends** and **making the most of the friendships you already have.** You'll find tips, quizzes, and even advice and stories from girls just like you.

Having friends who understand and appreciate you for who you are is what it's all about—finding friends who are **really right for you.** We hope this book helps you do just that.

Your friends at American Girl

Making Friends

Making a new friend takes time and even a little courage, but it's worth it because good friends are like . . .

♥ a sunny day. (Friends make life happier.)

♥ an umbrella in the rain. (Friends make gloomy days brighter.)

♥ a pile of autumn leaves. (Friends make things more fun.)

Friend Finders

Sometimes it just takes being in the right place at the right time to find a friend. Get involved in activities you enjoy, and you'll improve your chances of meeting someone to enjoy them with.

Join a club
In Girl Scouts, 4-H, and other after-school groups, you'll work on projects together and, chances are, find friends, too.

Take a class
Sign up for swimming, computers, or dance. You'll be surrounded by people to meet, and you'll learn something new!

Start something

What are you into? If it's reading, start a book club. If it's chess, start a chess club. Try to get girls together who like the same thing, and it's almost sure to pay off. Ask your teacher or librarian to help you get something going.

Play a sport

Join the team! Regular practices and exciting games can lead to close friendships.

Just get out of the house!

Watch for other opportunities to get together with girls in your community, church, or school. Put yourself in situations where you might meet people, and, hey, you just might!

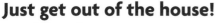

Conversation Starters

When it comes to making new friends, you have to get the conversation started. Here are some ways to get talking:

Just introduce yourself!

Hi! I'm Alisha. Are you signing up for dance?

Find something in common

I saw you at the concert. Do you like jazz, too?

Offer to help

I can show you where that classroom is.

Could someone be trying to get to know you better?

Try to keep the conversation going.

Once you've had a conversation, don't let it stop there. Look for chances to talk again. The more you talk, the more you'll get to know if this girl might be a good friend for you.

When You're Shy

Shy Shy Shy Shy

For some girls, walking up to someone they don't know is no big deal. For other girls, it's really hard. And, unfortunately, shyness can sometimes be mistaken for unfriendliness by other girls.

She's not talking to me. Does that mean she doesn't want to be friends with me?

Meeting new friends, especially when you're shy, takes confidence and determination. It's kind of like climbing a big mountain. But with every risk you take, no matter how small, **you're getting closer** to meeting some great girls and enjoying fun friendships.

Here are some tips for speaking up:

⚙ **Approach a person rather than a whole group,** and act as natural as you can. Be prepared by bringing extra pencils, tissues, or gum. Offering to share is a great way to start talking to someone.

⚙ **Let your body help you talk.** It's hard to have a conversation with a girl whose head is down or whose arms are crossed tightly across her chest. So take a deep breath, relax, and smile.

⚙ **Just get those first words out!** Don't wait until you feel totally comfortable to approach someone. Take some risks. Say something simple like, "Hi. How are you?" You may be surprised by how easy it is to go from there. Remember, most people are flattered when someone shows an interest in them. Try to let others know you're interested in what they have to say.

14

⚙ Practice at home in front of a mirror. Just act like you're talking to someone you've never met. It might sound silly, but it works. Once you have said the words to yourself over and over, saying them to someone else won't be as difficult.

⚙ Ask your mom or dad to help you practice, practice, practice. The more you speak up, the more natural it will feel. Try out conversation starters at the dinner table. Order for yourself at restaurants, and ask questions of salespeople. After a while, speaking up won't seem so hard.

15

Advice from Girls

Here's what girls had to say about making new friends:

"Walk up to someone who is alone, not with a group of friends. She will be glad someone is talking to her!"

Sarah, age 10

"I try my best to be kind, honest, and loyal. Then I just trust that friendships will happen, and so far they have."

Elizabeth, age 11

"Making friends is a lot like doing a jigsaw puzzle. Some people fit in a certain place and others don't. Just don't try to force it."

Ryan, age 14

16

"Don't judge people by what other people say about them. Get to know them, then decide for yourself!"

Sam, age 13

"I sit back and watch people for a while. If they seem nice from a distance, then I start talking to them."

Natalie, age 9

"The number one thing about making friends is to be yourself. Don't try to be someone you're not. People won't respect you if they think you're a faker."

Amanda, age 13

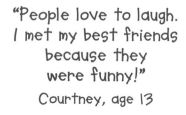

"People love to laugh. I met my best friends because they were funny!"

Courtney, age 13

Trying Too Hard?

What doesn't work with friends? Clinging. Friendships can end *fast* when one person feels overwhelmed by the other. In other words, don't try too hard!

What rates high on the **cling-o-meter?**

You meet your new friend on Monday. On Wednesday, you ask her to be your best friend.

cling-o-meter rating:

When friendships are new, it's important to let them grow naturally. Don't rush into making the friendship more than it is. For now, just focus on getting to know your friend better.

Your friend has told you she can't come over, but you really, really want her to. You don't understand why she doesn't want to come over, so you call her—again and again.

cling-o-meter rating:

Yikes! Take a deep breath. Respect is a key part of friendship, and you're not respecting your friend's wishes. Give her some space, and invite another friend over instead.

You see your friend out bike riding with another girl. You're so upset that you cry for an hour and refuse to talk to her the next morning on the bus.

cling-o-meter rating:

Just because she has other friends doesn't mean she doesn't care for you, and trying to make her feel guilty is more likely to hurt your friendship than make it better. Instead, reassure yourself that your friend is still your friend, and remind yourself that you have other friends, too.

Careful. Your presents may make your friend feel too much pressure, and that could change an otherwise good friendship. Also, you won't know whether your friend likes you for you or for all the gifts you give her. So cool it on the spending, and think of other ways to let your friend know you care about her.

cling-o-meter rating:

You've been friends for a few months. For four weeks in a row, you've spent your allowance on presents for your new friend.

Circle of Friends

20

Rather than searching for that one perfect friend, surround yourself with many friends. You'll bring out the best in one another!

Do you dream of that one *perfect* best friend—the girl who will meet your every friendship need?

The truth is, **no one person can meet all your needs.** Besides, that's way too much pressure to put on one person!

Instead of waiting and hoping for the perfect friend to come along, try to build a **circle of friends.** Don't limit yourself to people who seem just like you. Maybe there's an older or younger girl in your neighborhood you'd like to get to know better—or even a boy you've met.

Be open to all kinds of friendships. One friend might be great at listening but not like the same hobbies you do. And you might have another friend who's really fun but isn't so easy to be serious with.

How do you know if someone will be a good friend? At first, you don't. One girl may look or dress like you, but when you're with her, it just doesn't feel right. Another girl may seem totally different from you, but you feel like you can really be yourself with her.

Just remember, **each of your friends has something unique to offer you.** What's most important is that you—and all your friends—bring out the best in one another.

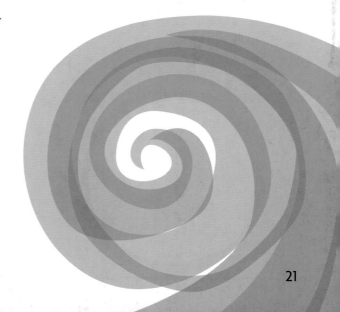

all Kinds of Friends

Try your best to build a good balance of buds.

True-blue friend

This friend has seen you at your best and your worst, and she loves you just the same. You can talk to her about anything at any time, or you can just sit silently with her and still feel comfortable. This girl will be your friend till the end.

True-blue friend qualities

- Great for a pep talk
- Makes you feel 100% comfortable when you are with her
- Picks you up when you are down
- Won't judge you
- Knows you inside and out

Giggling girl

This friend is just plain fun! When you're with her, you giggle at the silliest things. If you're feeling down, she'll have you rolling on the floor laughing in no time.

Giggling girl qualities

- Makes you laugh (and laugh and laugh . . .)
- Takes a bad situation and turns it around by making you smile
- Turns the most boring activity into a ton of fun
- Always entertains you

Go-to girl

Every girl needs a friend she can turn to when she needs some advice. Maybe this friend is your big sister, your neighbor, or a family friend. She tells you what she thinks is best for you, even if it's not what you want to hear. She always makes you feel as if everything will be O.K.

Go-to girl qualities

- Honest and straightforward when giving you advice
- 100% trustworthy
- Has a good perspective on any problems you have
- Cares about what's best for you

Casual pal

This friend shares an interest with you. Maybe you're on the same soccer team or take dance lessons together. The two of you might hang out only at your shared activities, but when you're together, it's great. Just make sure that you don't keep score on who's better at what-ever you have in common. Be supportive, and keep it fun.

Casual pal qualities

- Shares your interests
- Gets you outside of your normal group of friends
- Motivates you to practice more

23

Faraway friend

You and this girl have stayed close, even though she's far away. You don't have to talk every day to stay friends, but hearing from her makes you smile. You always pick up right where you left off, and if you get to visit each other, it's nothing but fun!

Delightfully different friend

There's never a dull moment with this friend because she isn't just like you. Maybe she's from a different culture, or maybe she's a *he*. This friend challenges you to be creative and try new things.

Faraway friend qualities

- Helps you learn about life in a different place
- Brightens your day with an e-mail or a postcard
- Brings a fresh and fair perspective to your problems since she doesn't know all your friends

Delightfully different friend qualities

- Has interests that are not the same as yours
- Encourages you to try new ways of doing things
- Makes you think, "Oh, I never thought of it that way!"

Close-to-home friend

This friend is one that's easy to take for granted. It might be a sibling, a cousin, a parent, or a grandparent. Our family members are our *forever* friends.

Close-to-home friend qualities

- Is always there
- Knows you inside and out
- Loves you no matter what!

Furry friend

This friend might be your pet dog, your neighbor's kitty, or even your favorite stuffed animal. No matter what she is, she's the one who listens to you and never judges you. She might not give you any advice, but one look at her fuzzy face makes you smile.

Furry friend qualities

- Never tells your secrets
- Comes when you call her
- Stays by your side

Getting to Know Her

Learning more about each other can help you decide whether your friendship will flourish or fizzle. But sometimes, when you are getting to know a person, it's hard to find things to talk about. Avoid awkward moments by playing these get-to-know-you games.

Big
important point:

When you first meet someone, **try hard NOT to rely on gossip** to fill up the conversation. It might be tempting, but it almost always backfires and sends a message to your new friend that you're not very trustworthy.

You		
Winter	or	**summer**
Ice cream	or	**french fries**
Shopping	or	**slumber parties**
Sports events	or	**plays**
Art class	or	**gym class**
Hotels	or	**camping**
Inline skating	or	**biking**
On the stage	or	**in the audience**
Pants	or	**skirts**
Dogs	or	**cats**
Talking it out	or	**writing it down**
Board games	or	**movies**

Me		
Winter	or	**summer**
Ice cream	or	**french fries**
Shopping	or	**slumber parties**
Sports events	or	**plays**
Art class	or	**gym class**
Hotels	or	**camping**
Inline skating	or	**biking**
On the stage	or	**in the audience**
Pants	or	**skirts**
Dogs	or	**cats**
Talking it out	or	**writing it down**
Board games	or	**movies**

27

"Things About Me" Game

* Find a deck of playing cards.

* Take turns picking a card from the deck. The number on the card tells you how many interesting facts about yourself to share. If you pick a three, you might say:

* If you pick the joker, ask your friend a question of your choice.

* If you pick a face card, answer a question from your friend or from the next page.

"I once rode an elephant."

"I love to swim."

"I have a rock collection."

Big important point:

Nobody should have to answer a question she finds too embarrassing. You always have the option to say "pass."

Questions to cut out and share!

What is your favorite food?

What book character is most like you? Why?

If you could be any animal,
what would you be?

What's your favorite kind of music?

What is your dream job?

Name one great thing about your family.

What is something you are scared of?

What is your favorite part of the school day?

Tell about your greatest adventure ever.

If you were given a million dollars,
what would you do with it?

If you could change your name,
what would it be?

Name something you've always wanted
to do but haven't had the chance to do.

What is your all-time favorite movie?

Name a family tradition you enjoy.

If you could go anywhere in the world,
where would it be?

What word best describes you?

True Friendship Story

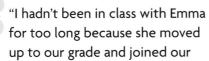

> **A real friend is one who walks in when the rest of the world walks out.**
> —Walter Winchell

"I hadn't been in class with Emma for too long because she moved up to our grade and joined our class late. She seemed nice, but we never got to know each other. To be honest, I was a little scared by how smart she was. I mean, she skipped a whole grade!

Anyway, we were in class, and I was reading aloud in our small group. I accidentally missed a word. It had a weird ending, and I didn't read it the right way.

That's when Maggie, another girl in my group, embarrassed me by saying loudly, 'The word is *buffet*. Duh! You didn't know *buffet*?'

I felt so bad, I just wanted to run away.

Just then, out of nowhere, Emma piped up and said, 'Maggie, you miss plenty of words. You have no right to make fun of someone else.' I was stunned. The whole group was stunned. And Maggie, who is used to getting away with rude comments, was stunned, too. Suddenly the teacher spoke up, and we all returned to our seats.

I mouthed 'thank you' to Emma.

I couldn't wait until lunch to thank her. I let her know how much I respected her for what she had done. We played all recess and most recesses after. She's still one of the best friends I have ever had.

—An American girl

P.S. Maggie was a lot less rude from then on, too."

Making Friendships Last

Great friendships take **time, patience,** and a little bit of **hard work.**

Being friends is like riding a bicycle. Sometimes the ride feels smooth and easy, but other times, you hit bumps in the road. You have to steer carefully and pedal hard to make sure that you stay on the right path. But in the end, friendship is usually worth the ride.

Keep
pedaling

umps
head

Smell
the
flowers

Go
back

Trouble Starters

You won't be able to avoid every fight with your friends. You'll have fewer fights, though, if you steer clear of these trouble starters.

Top ten trouble starters

1. Talking about someone behind her back

2. Asking a friend to take sides and choose between you and another friend

3. Breaking a promise or telling a secret

4. Being bossy

5. Bragging or showing off

6. Leaving someone out—and letting her know it in a mean way

7. Being jealous of or competing with your friend

8. Saying something unkind about your friend or her loved ones

9. Embarrassing your friend in front of others

10. Being too busy to listen

Really Listening

It's easy to do the talking when your friend is a good listener, but being a good listener is hard. Think of a conversation as being like a ride on a teeter-totter. Have you ever been on a teeter-totter with someone who wouldn't let you down? That's how it feels when one person does all the talking. It's no fun!

A good conversation goes something like this:

First your friend shares . . .

. . . and then you comment on what she shared so that she knows you were listening . . .

Try these listening tips the next time you talk with a friend:

✳ When your friend is talking, your **eyes** should be on her, and your **brain** should be paying attention to her words—not focusing on your next point.

✳ Try not to interrupt. No one likes feeling cut off. If you don't understand something, **wait for her to finish,** and then ask a question.

I see your point.

Could you explain that again?

✳ Try not to judge your friend, even if you don't agree with how she's handling a problem. **Consider her point of view.**

✳ Offer **support** with comments such as, "Wow, that must have made you really mad," or "You must have been so happy!"

Hmm, I never thought about it that way.

How were you feeling? Did that make you mad?

Big important point: Sometimes, when a friend has a serious problem, you might need to do lots of listening—and less sharing. This is O.K. as long as it doesn't happen all the time. When your friend does need you, listen to her, and take comfort in knowing that she'll do the same for you when you need her.

Building Trust

When someone tells you something private, it's as if they're giving you a compliment. They are telling you that they trust you and value your opinion.

If someone trusts you with confidential information, you need to keep it private. If you don't, you risk losing one of the most important parts of a friendship—trust.

When two people trust each other, they have opened the doors for their friendship to grow stronger. If you break your friend's trust, it's like slamming that door shut.

Think about it:

Do you really want to trade the respect of your friend for a moment of attention? People may like to hear gossip, but the truth is, they don't trust—or respect—the person spreading it. So if someone trusts you enough to share something personal with you, **keep your lips zipped.**

SSShhhh

REALLY Big

important point: There is only one exception to this rule: If your friend is in danger, you need to tell an adult—not your other friends. It's always the right decision to keep a friend safe. Even if she's upset at first, in the end, she'll know that you were looking out for her and that you cared.

Being There

A big part of friendship is being in your friend's corner when she needs you. Here are two ways to stick up for a friend when other kids are giving her trouble.

1. Let the others know with words that it's not O.K. to pick on your friend. This works especially well if you have the support of your other friends, too. And while it may seem daring and even scary to stand up to a rude classmate, it shows that you're a strong person and a loyal friend.

Hey, that wasn't very nice! I can't believe you just said that!

2. If standing up to a classmate doesn't feel comfortable, let a grown-up know that your friend is being picked on. Tell the grown-up that you are concerned for your friend, and give examples of what you have seen happening.

Ms. Johnson, I'm worried for my friend. She has been getting bullied by . . .

Mrs. King, I think you should know about something . . .

If talking to a grown-up seems too big a step, you could write an anonymous note or even ask your parents to talk to someone for you. One way or another, let those in charge know what is happening so that they can take care of it.

Big important point: Talking to a grown-up is NOT tattling—it is being a good friend and bystander and reporting behavior that is NOT O.K.

Remember: This is a time when your friend really needs you, so don't be afraid to let her know how much you disagree with the hurtful things that were said.

Quiz! Fighting Fair

Sometimes you can't avoid a fight. But do you know how to fight right? Read each fighting strategy, and decide whether it's fair or unfair. Circle your choice.

1. If you talk really loudly and even cry, you'll get your point across better.

2. Talk about the problem to everyone except your friend. Get lots of people on your side so that your friend will give in faster.

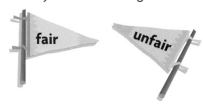

3. Don't talk about why you're angry. You shouldn't have to tell your friend. She should already know.

4. When your friend is talking, don't focus on what she's saying. Instead, use the time to think about what you're going to say next.

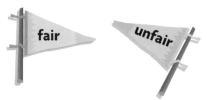

5. Make sure you bring up everything your friend has ever done that bothers you—not just what you are unhappy about now.

6. The silent treatment is better than arguing. A cold shoulder will cause your friend to warm up fast!

Answers

How did you answer? If you said **unfair** to all of the statements on the last page, you know that to untangle the knots and solve your friendship troubles, you need a **good attitude** and some **basic ground rules.** Here they are:

1. Cool it. Shouting and tears will get a person's attention, but they also keep that person from understanding the real reason you're upset. Try to express yourself as calmly as you can. Remember: words said in anger can really hurt. Hurtful words only make the problem bigger. Instead, cool down. Say what you mean and mean what you say, but don't say it mean.

2. Keep it private. Talking to others can help you sort out your feelings, but it's no substitute for talking directly to the person you're mad at. Don't put others in the middle of your argument.

3. Say what's bothering you. Don't expect your friend to read your mind. She can't change or fix the problem if she doesn't know what it is. Ask a parent or another trusted adult to help you sort out your feelings. You'll be much better prepared when you do try to talk it out.

4. Pay attention. It's hard to listen when you're angry. But your friend may be trying to tell you something important that could change how you feel. If you hear it soon enough, you can often stop a fight before it gets worse.

5. Stick to today. Bringing up things from the past or starting up old arguments takes the attention away from what's happening now and only stirs up more bad feelings. Focus on solving one problem at a time.

6. Don't clam up. Some people deal with arguments by changing the subject or pretending there isn't a problem. Ignoring the problem—or your friend—won't make things better.

Big important point: Nobody's perfect. Everybody makes mistakes. If you expect your friends to be perfect, you'll always be disappointed. So if you're angry with a friend, ask yourself if she really meant to hurt you or if she just made a mistake.

Talking It Out

Are you ready to hear each other out? If so, all you need is a quiet place and the willingness to work together. Remember these helpful hints:

1. One of the hardest parts about fixing things after a fight is getting started. **Don't be afraid to make the first move.** It doesn't mean you're giving in or letting your friend "win." Nobody wins if you never speak again.

Here are some ways to get the conversation started:

I'm still angry, but I care about our friendship and want to work things out.

I feel terrible about how we ended things.

I'm ready to talk if you want to.

Notice that all the sentences start with **"I."** That's because you're sharing your feelings—not telling her what she should have done differently. Using "I" statements gets the conversation off to a good start.

2. The more you listen to your friend, the more she'll want to listen to you. Agree to **take turns talking** so that you both get a chance to say what's on your mind.

3. **Name the problem.** Keep using statements starting with "I." These are *your* feelings you're talking about. And try to avoid saying "you always" or "you never." Chances are, those statements aren't true, and they will just make your friend angry.

4. You know how you feel, but **put yourself in your friend's place.** Try to understand why she acted the way she did.

5. **Make an agreement** about how to handle things in the future. Maybe you've learned something about each other. Try to figure out what that is so that you don't have the same fight again.

6. You can **agree to disagree.** You might both be sorry about what happened and still not agree on everything. It's O.K. to have different opinions.

Big important point: It's almost always worth it to try to work things out. Even if you've decided you and a friend aren't a great match, you can remain friends—just not close ones.

Making Things Right

If a problem between friends is very small, a simple "Sorry about that!" might be enough to get things back to normal. But if the fight between you and your friend is a big one—and you're the one who needs to apologize—take a deep breath and do it with words that are clear and from the heart.

Follow these simple rules for saying you're sorry:

 Say the words: "I'm sorry for . . ."

 Reassure your friend that **you won't repeat the mistake,** and let her know what you wish you had done instead:
"I won't do that again. Next time I'll . . ."

 Let her know that the friendship means a lot to you and that **you want to make things right:**
"Is there anything I can do to make you feel better?"

important point: Never be too proud to ask for forgiveness—or too stubborn to give it. If someone asks you to forgive her, she's done what she can to make things right. If you need to apologize for your part in the argument, do it. Then put the fight behind you and start rebuilding your friendship.

True Friendship Story

"Danielle and I were on the same gymnastics team. We spent long hours together at the gym and got along great. *Finally*, I thought, *the friendship I've always dreamed of.*

Then one day everything changed.

New levels for gymnastics teams came out, and Danielle moved up a level. I didn't. I was crushed and cried all afternoon. I felt sure the days of our perfect friendship were over. I blamed myself for not being a better gymnast.

I felt hurt and even angry at Danielle for being able to do more in the gym. To make matters worse, it was becoming clear that gymnastics just wasn't for me, and I ended up dropping from the team altogether.

Then, one lonely afternoon, the phone rang. It was Danielle saying how much she missed our friendship. I was so happy because I had missed her, too. We got together that day and came up with a plan to build back our friendship. We even asked our moms for help. Now Danielle's mom drops her off at my house in the morning so that we can walk to school together.

We've worked hard to find time to be together, and as a result, our friendship has grown. In fact, it's stronger than it's ever been. For us, gymnastics brought us together, but true friendship—and determination—kept us that way."

—An American girl

Celebrating Friendship

Think of a friendship as being like a beaded necklace. Every experience you and your friend have together— every memory you make—is like a bead.

Bead by bead, the two of you create something beautiful. And like a precious necklace, your friendship is something you'll cherish and want to take care of.

ping

soccer

school play

skating

talking

music

craft

sleepovers

movies

lunches

dance

riding
bikes

homewo

Showing You Care

Friendship is a two-way street—you care for her and she cares for you back. Here are some great ways to show your friend how much she matters:

Help make her birthday special.

Stop what you're doing and listen if she needs you.

Give her half your snack if she forgets hers.

Give her a pep talk if she needs it.

Call her to keep in touch, especially through busy times.

Wish her good luck on a test.

Always tell her if she has something stuck in her teeth or if her zipper is down.

Be happy for her if she wins something.

Tell her when she looks nice.

If she calls you, call her back.

Introduce her to new friends.

Trust her with your true feelings.

If she's having a bad day, send her a note.

Teach her to do something you know how to do.

Let her teach you something new.

Lend her a pencil if she forgets hers.

Give her a small gift.

Make her a picture or write her a letter.

If you know she collects something and you see one, get it for her.

Tell her you care about her.

Give her a hug if she's upset.

Save her a seat.

Help her if she's having trouble.

Let her borrow something.

Stand up for her.

Keep her secrets.

Return what you borrow from her.

Tell her a joke to make her laugh.

Laugh at her jokes.

Say thank you when she does something nice.

Tell an adult if you think she is in danger.

Be reliable and on time.

Help her clean her room.

Remember her favorite things.

If she forgets her mittens, give her one of yours.

If you have something good in your lunch, share it!

Never let her sit alone . . . unless she wants to.

When you're done reading a good book, offer to let her read it.

Invite her over.

Stop her if she's cutting herself down.

Notice if she gets her hair cut.

Be nice to her brothers and sisters.

Go to her games or recitals.

If she's not in school, call and check on her.

Tell her why you admire her.

Listen without judging.

Smile whenever you see her.

61

Friendship Ties

The more time you spend with a friend, the more opportunities you have to create lasting memories. Over time, you'll develop certain things you and your friend often do together. These **traditions** become an important part of your friendship, strengthening the bond between the two of you.

Want to start some traditions with a friend? Here's how:

1 **Pick something you both love to do.** It could be something as simple as watching the same TV show and talking about it, or doing something special for each other's birthdays. Maybe it's going to the same place together once a year.

2 **Remember the tradition.** The activity you're sharing with your friend can become a tradition only if you repeat it over and over, and that takes some *effort*. But that's also what makes it so special!

Big important point: "Inside jokes" happen when friends who shared a funny moment are reminded of it later. These jokes are a fun way to bring back memories and enjoy a good laugh, but inside jokes can also make others feel left out. Unless you plan to let others in on the joke, avoid mentioning it when they're around.

Here are some girls' favorite friendship traditions:

"My friend Annie and I have always had tea parties in the spring, and we give each other little gifts and take pictures. In all the pictures, we are laughing and having fun!"

Katie, 10

"My friends and I have 'Watermelon Wednesday' when we all wear pink and green."

Shelby, 10

"We met at summer camp and became pen pals. Every time one of us writes, the other returns a letter right away. Every year we go to camp together and have a reunion!"

Katy, 9, and Kelsey, 9

tea time

"Our tradition is called 'Sister Day.' My friend and I dress alike and pretend that we are sisters for the day."

Morgan, 9

"When we were little, my friend and I had our picture taken with the Easter Bunny at the mall. Now that we are older, we still go every year. It's fun to look back at the pictures and see how we have changed."

Nan, 9

"I have a friend who moved across town, but we still get to see each other because every spring we pick blueberries and every fall we pick apples. We always spend our birthdays together, too."

Grace, 8

65

Friendship Fun

Try these ideas for keeping the fun in your friendship!

✳ Make a **time capsule** to open together in five or ten years. Write down your dreams and your predictions for the future. Include a description of life as you know it. Put in letters from parents or friends, ticket stubs, and anything else that's important to you today. Seal it up and store it in a safe place!

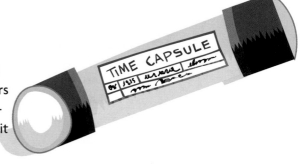

✳ Write and publish a **newsletter** for your friends and families. You can include stories, pictures, artwork, poetry, jokes, and anything else that you and your friend—and your readers—find interesting!

✳ Write, direct, and produce your own show. Invite people you know to attend. Try to make a video of your production!

✳ Sign up to take part in a **charity race.** Train for it together, and collect donations. Whether you're helping to find a cure for a disease or raising awareness of a problem in your area, you'll be making a difference!

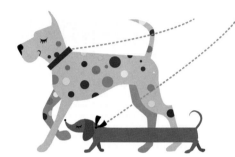

✳ Start a **business** together. It could be weeding gardens or walking dogs. Create fun flyers, and ask your neighbors or others you know to be customers. Do something special with the money you earn!

✳ Make a **scrapbook.** Fill it with photos, drawings, and other mementos of your friendship.

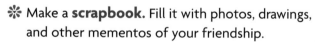

✳ Invent your own board game. Have your friends and families try it out.

✳ Help each other clean and organize your rooms. You might even be able to rearrange the furniture—with a parent's permission, of course. With a friend's help, a big job is somehow easier and much more fun. Be sure to take "before" and "after" pictures!

Friendship Crafts

Get creative! Try these crafts with friends, or surprise them with a gift that celebrates your friendship.

Perfect Picture of Friendship

You'll need:
- Pencil
- Large piece of foam-core board
- Patterned paper or ribbon
- Glue
- Pictures, quotes, and mementos
- Sparkly stickers or plastic gemstones
- Cord or yarn
- Stapler or tape

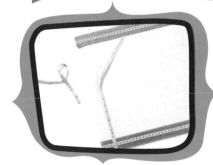

1. Draw a faint line 1 to 3 inches in from each edge of the foam-core board. This marks your "frame." Glue ribbon or strips of brightly colored or patterned paper onto the frame.

2. In the middle of the frame, make a collage with pictures, quotes, and mementos of your friendship, such as movie tickets or school programs. Fill the gaps with stickers, gemstones, or other decorative items.

3. Tie a knot at each end of the cord or yarn. Turn the foam-core over, and center the cord at the top. Staple or tape both ends of the cord, just above the knots. Now hang up your masterpiece!

MARIAH JORDAN

Sleepover Memory Pillow

You'll need:

- Plain pillowcase
- Cardboard
- Fabric markers
- Friendship quotes

1. Place a piece of cardboard inside the pillowcase so that the marker will not bleed through to the other side.

2. Pull the pillowcase tightly across the cardboard. Use fabric markers to decorate the edges of the pillowcase with fun designs, such as stars, hearts, or flowers. Add quotes about friendship, if you like.

3. Leave room so that when friends sleep over, they can sign their names or write something about your friendship.

Note: When you wash the pillowcase, follow the manufacturer's instructions on your fabric markers.

True Friendship Story

Friendship is a sheltering tree.
—Samuel Taylor Coleridge

"It was like any other day—I was at home, just hanging out, and I went to the garage to get something. When I opened the door, all I could see were flames. I was frantic! I ran to the neighbors. We called the fire department, but then, all we could do was wait. I watched everything my family owned burn to the ground.

I was devastated. The sadness I felt is hard to describe. I was sad about so many things, but my mom says one of the first things I said was, 'My doll. I lost my doll.'

The next few days were kind of a blur, but one thing I remember is my friends. They just kept on coming, bringing us food and clothes.

But one friend really surprised me. It was two days after the fire, and my mom and I were rummaging through the remains of our house. My friend Wendy walked up. She had moved a few months before and now lived two hours away. When our eyes met, I was overjoyed. I couldn't believe she had come all that way.

Wendy handed me a long box. When I opened it, my heart skipped a beat. It was Wendy's doll like mine and a whole bunch of clothes for her. 'I want you to have her' was all she said. Then we hugged each other for a long time.

I was so touched, I didn't know what to say.

I will never forget the feeling I had that day or what Wendy did for me. The doll and my friend will always have a place in my heart."

—An American girl

By now, you know how important friendship is. Next to our families, our friends know us best.

If you already have a circle of friends who make you happy, you are truly lucky. **Cherish your friends and try to be the kind of friend you would want to have.**

If you haven't found that great circle of friends yet, keep looking. Work to be the best friend you can be, and use what you've learned in this book to choose wisely and **be patient while your friendships grow.**

Remember: Some friendships will last a long time and others will fade away, but every friendship will teach you a little bit more about life and about **the very best friend you have . . .**

Good-Friend Checklist

Now that you've read the book, you know what it takes to make friends and to be a good friend. Are you being the best friend that you can be? Put an X next to the statements that sound like you.

☐ I am reliable. When I say I'm going to do something, I do it.

☐ I try hard to be a good listener.

☐ I stick up for my friends when others say bad things about them.

☐ I let my friends get to know the real me.

☐ I refuse to say bad things about my friends, even when they make mistakes.

☐ If I am angry with a friend, I tell her and we work it out.

☐ When my friends cut themselves down, I disagree with them.

☐ I ask for support when I need it.

☐ I am honest with my friends and say things in a kind way.

☐ If I hurt someone's feelings, I apologize.

☐ I keep my friends' personal information private.

How did you do? Which areas of friendship are hardest for you? What do you need to do differently? Finish this sentence: "Starting today, I will be a better friend by

_____

_____

_____

_____

_____"

How did you meet your best friends?

Write to us!

Send your true friendship stories to:
Friends Editor
American Girl
8400 Fairway Place
Middleton, WI 53562

All comments and suggestions received by American Girl may be used without compensation or acknowledgment. Sorry—photos can't be returned.

What special traditions do you share?

Do you have any secrets for making friendships last?

Here are some other American Girl books you might like:

❏ I read it.

❏ I read it.

❏ I read it.

❏ I read it.

❏ I read it.

❏ I read it.

Friendship Posters

Celebrate friendship with these
tear-out mini posters.
Hang them in your room
or in your locker, and share
a few with friends!